GIVERS & TAKERS 2

GIVERS
&
TAKERS
· 2 ·

POEMS BY

Jane Mayhall

THE EAKINS PRESS
NEW YORK

Grateful acknowledgement for permission to reprint poems is made to the editors of the following publications: *Aphra*, 'Tracing Back'; *Descant*, 'Death of a Prize Poet'; *Event*, 'Plums and Pears' and 'New Couples'; *Mill Mountain Review*, 'Disposal Grounds'; *The Nation*, 'Nightmares'; *New York Quarterly Review*, 'The Young Man'; *The New York Times*, 'On the Meaning of Literary Influence' and 'Critic's Choice'; *Perspective*, 'Pigs'; *Southern Humanities Review*, 'For the Gifted' and 'Insanity is too Simple'; *Wormwood Review*, 'Thoughts at Midnight.' 'The Human Animal' is from *Ready for the Ha Ha*; 'Givers & Takers,' 'Notes for That Big Gold Book' and 'The Subway Church' from *Givers & Takers 1* (1966 and 1968—Eakins Press).

SBN cloth 0–87130–032–x
paper 0–87130–032–8
Library of Congress Catalog Card Number 68–55445

For John Evarts, *a giver*

CONTENTS

GIVERS & TAKERS

Out of your side eye you see them,
the givers and takers, the killers
or sustainers. Quiet at the wheel;
or at the pitch of erratic traffic
some vent their cruelties
in the guise of acceptable accident.
"We can't help that it happened!"
Or, those who helped to avoid.
The generous flinch in the stomach;
or, the eyeball craving blood.

Some men, seeming bloodless as steel,
were shaping the gentle enactment.
Others, oozing good neighbor appeal,
were planning the mordant assault.
Our causes are puzzles in crises.
But, look to veiled wishes in air.
We help, or we hate; we give or we take.
Slice havoc. Or mop up despair.

THOUGHTS AT MIDNIGHT

Arbitration is a secondary impulse;
the delight at being alive, at having
survived the horrendous adventures may still
be entitled that (loveably, and adhering
to interstices of the momentary) word:
Gratitude. In literature, it becomes
style. In politics, expenditure.
In religion, ecstasy. But how
about day-to-day living?

Failure is the preservation
of Quality.

Idle thought!
Idle America!
Useless commerce . . .
which every country
must keep imitating.

WHEN LIBERTY HAS BECOME A PRISON CRYING *ME*

Who plays the magic number,
which is chaos into squalor;
and my dear feminists
ad-libbed and vulgar;
and my dear masculinists
beating up their brothers;
and they dance and squawk together;
and the world, as ever was it,
takes work from those who give it,
and lives to make demands,
with pejorative, idle minds;
and fists, their symbol hands;
but the carols of naked bones
still interlace the stones;
and William Blake died in a scroll of dreams.

STICK-IN-THE-MUD

The stick is alive,
  it comprehends the mud;
the mud coheres and holds
  the wavering stick.

(Half-green and ripped
  from stalk, it takes to
the bubbled sod, seeding out
  the tiny vernal plantings.)

But we, of bludgeoned mind,
  imagine, that like ourselves,
it represents a state
  of dead inaction . . . . . .

WE ARE GIVEN TWISTED

We are given twisted ideas about the majority.
Against this brutal, Puritanical age,
the heart is starving for pleasure.
Against leering public sex,
we are aching for the sensuality of kindness.
What do these robots, with their fissures,
dream of in the darkness? Unpaved vineyards
are in their closets, new balancing architectures.

CHRIST, you have made it;
your picture in *Chez Vogue*
out in front and a double-column
super star next to a "freaky blonde
dolly in a raggedy suede dress"
priced at $450, "in tone
of champagne, beige and brown."
Christ, you're part of
the Millennium, bearing the cross
to Calvary, attributed to Giorgione,
"product of futurity" and the ready-to-
wear "little spaghettini dress
and rayon bolero," Christ you
"delicious little powder puff
of a sta-dri swim cap."
And men still drink your blood,
excreting manna to the hungry mob.

INSANITY IS TOO SIMPLE

INSANITY is too simple.
To crazy people, everything
has a flaw, or looks horrible,
clear-bad, or is out to get them.
The paranoid is so certain, you
could call him stable, if the joke
appeals to you. It is sanity
that is complicated, seeing
the world as made of love, illogic
treading out its criss-cross
patterns. What brain can hold
a rainbow? What attitude survive
the facts? No crack-up wants to
accept life's not exact, but living
on the edge. The impossible, un-
determined, the pouring brims
of sanity.

NO MATTER HOW PHOTOGENIC ARE YOUR MOTIVES, I REFUSE TO SAY HURRAH FOR A CRIMINAL

WHAT I am sickened by in current criminality
is the piety. The two muggers I encountered had
that funny white suet look of the self-congratulatory,
their faces in that sanctimonious grin of the ulti-
mate philistine, feeling so damned justified, consoled
by the craven public image. "Look at me, Freud; look
at me, *Daily News*; look at me, psycho-poets; look at me
affluency's audience; look at me, *mon pere Genet*, cosy pries
in the citadels of *maudit*; I'm a good boy, good, good, good
and I pat myself on my nasty good head, for doing right
in the eyes of the All Virtuous Goody Bad; now I will
hit somebody with an iron pipe, or stab." And oh,
the glossy superior tone, yesterday, of the obscene crank
madman on the telephone; the curdling unctuousness!
the syrupy self-righteousness! The last time I heard
such a dedicated assault was among some ladies' aid type

women telling a preacher how much his sermon
                                    "meant"—close
to tears of exhibitionistic excitement. It's not a real
shock, is it? that thieves, rapists and murderers are the big-
sell cinema stars; their egos so preened and pious, they
don't challenge any part of us. We can worship, and smile,
and throw up, saying that everything is uniformly corrupt.
Perpetuating only a more hideous and fraudulent species,
the kind I would like to grimly satirize as Babbitts,
the fatuous members of the latest opportunists' clubs.

LINES, FROM A SPLIT CONNECTION

In times of stress, we have
the amplified obvious, like
watered-down Bach, and the switch-
on flak. I'll vote for it; but don't
want to have to listen to it . . . . . .

OH! WASHINGTON IRVING!

Oh! Washington Irving!
You never dreamed of advertising,
and the headless whoresman,
whoring.

DISPOSAL GROUNDS, FLORIDA

I AM inspired by the rubble of tomorrow,
in a backward grind, insoluble waste, rust,
iron guts, the cracked matted wings
of aeroplanes. Something perverse
within me hums, *tomorrow, tomorrow*;
for this pack of disintegration,
wrecked trailers, engines; and earth,
reposit for our junkmail slaughtered trees.
Compost, lime, shifts of dirty concrete;
I love this bitter monument. How best uphold,
erect a better time! Something within me
squeals, irrevocable, like rage; inalterable,
hateful future I embrace. Something within
me laughs, not despair; the heart
that knows this heart, the grass black
straight from nature; send out your
ardent, gritty tongue.

FOR THE CANDY MERCHANTS

Sorry! to me, pornographic books are scary
marshmallow; I don't want to get stuck in all
that goo. Though the subject matter seems
attractive, or like a kind of cake icing
with lots of preservative. But how about
murder pictures on newspaper stands? Better
or worse, these blood-lollypops? Give to
the inexpensive children.

Every revolution
  needs a religion against
which it rebels. Every
  child
needs a bad father to
  pronounce the bawdy squelch.
Every person has to be
  against.
And those who live in
  secular harmony
are just biding time.
  Two and two are seven;
little saints are hopping
  in between.

NIGHTMARES

I USED to really like my nightmares.
But now in the gut worry have given
up thought, and the image that makes
me growl and hang like a spectre
is the fact I'm waking up
in the nightmare of others.

TO A SUCCESSFUL HOW-TO POET

There's gravy in the groovy;
oiled and sugared gucky,
not to mention, there is money.
In all the appropriate crap
is how you've wrapped it up.
I note the selective trivia,
to catch the murky eyes;
like an ad-man's chopped Freud media,
you know what lures the flies.
My heart is sick, dispassionate.
I now recall your venom
when you spoke of a distinguished man,
who helped you to publication,

a damned good poet in his right
(he was about seventy-eight, or seventy-nine):
"Kick it, he's a square."
(And you were fifty-one.)
A year later you won a national prize
with your first bad poem.

THE RAW, HOT FEELING

SOAP is still better than detergents,
exercise is still better than sleeping pills,
love is still better than sex machines,
courtesy is still better than murder,
intelligence is still better than psychiatric labels,
Jesus is still better than Caesar,
trees are still better than plastic,
amity is still better than violence,
quality is still better than advertising,
dedicated work is still better than nihilism,
complication is still better than caricature,
all ages are better than group hostility,
art is still better than formlessness,
empathy is still better than indifference,

satisfaction is still better than entertainment,
clear thoughts are still better than drunkenness,
honesty is still better than success,
education is still better than war,
all races together are still better than one color,
walking is still better than jet planes;
the above list, for me, is letting off steam.
You won't believe it, the raw, hot feeling.

THE YOUNG MAN

I SAW a young black man who was a conductor
on Subway 7277, the Broadway local, walking
down the aisles picking up newspapers
and a lot of filthy things people had thrown
around, picking them up with his two bare hands
(he had a slim face, and a self-respecting,
    avoiding eye)
carrying them back near to his box compartment,
arranging neatly at the side to put into some
    waste basket
later, not extending the process, and returning to
his box in time for the next local station.

X-RATED POEMS FOR CHILDREN

Baby Rae
Baby Rae has a chicken,
the chicken is black and white.
Baby Rae likes the chicken.
The chicken thinks Baby
Rae is stupid. There is no
reason the chicken thinks.

Moma
See Moma. She has a dress.
Hit her with a church
steeple.

Tomorrow

Tomorrow I'm going to play
with all the famous poets.
Ha-ha. Bang-bang; we make
out easy. We say thing things
backwards. We steal CHOCO-
up-date from the ice-
box. Please give me a new
clothes hanger to sleep in.

The Circus

Spontaneous allegory.
I am two years old at the circus.
I petted a trick worm.
He bit me.

Lunch Basket

Oh let us go and fall
in the lunch basket. See the funny
people; birthdays have one day;
con men fly like witch-bane in
the garden. There is no end to no-
where. Superficialities, hug me,
tell, tell, tell
another name.

THE UNNAMED

So you dropped straight down from the
    ceiling,
so you are sitting on my head like a golden
garnet insect, caught accidentally in the heat
of my search for you. Did I want to save you?
I cupped my hand over your frail wing; and
    felt

no tremor of resistance. But I was afraid
of the hurt you might die of. Just for this,
you fall to the rug; my insensible hopelessness
that has no pattern. How lucky I am to see you!
How lucky I am to free you! you gentle of
    mystification,
pulsing like rain. I lift you once more in my hand,
and open the night window outside. The
    darkness
will save us both. And you are gone . . . . .

THE homosexual upheaval
is all too tongue-in-chic;
pardon! but the congenital
exploitation takes the daring
out of its natural setting.
The magic of privacy looms
between the television programs;
while the madness of getting
your money's worth (planted as
the advertising bait) is exhaling
a bad name, faggot pollution;
and those who were are not, and say
they might. But it's nothing based
on love, this passive merchandise,
and denigrates like sign-board
fingers pointing. So, those who'd
keep their roots go underground.

YOUNG pigs and old pigs,
pigs eating popcorn,
pigs carrying knives,
pigs combing their long golden hair.
Pigs dousing themselves with deodorant,
pigs writing plays,
pigs burning down libraries,
pigs walking, pigs sitting,
pigs asleep in a meadow;
pigs working in offices,
pigs drop-out,
pigs in school,
pigs running the government,
pigs shouting through a bull horn;
pigs with pig noses,
pigs with horse noses,
female pigs,
male pigs,

old pigs,
young pigs.
Pigs in a cradle,
pigs making bombs,
pigs urinating in gutters,
pigs with hair;
bald-headed pigs,
pigs making a living,
pigs not making a living;
parasite pigs,
establishment pigs;
yesterday I looked at
myself in a mirror;
there was a pig in each eye,
both of them said to me
"why don't you go back where
you came from, you fraud?"

WHOEVER

WHOEVER takes responsibility
gets the blame.

TO A FRIEND IN BEREAVEMENT

DEATH is such a shock,
it makes you want to bite somebody.
Here's my good arm, friend;
take a nip.

FROM THE GENERAL ASSEMBLY

IF his motives are evil,
forgive his faults.
If his intent is well-meaning,
forgive him nothing.

TELEVISION DÉCOR

MURDER is the kicky ornament
to make your little room a chic palliative
against thinking for yourself, but accept
the corny puff, big-faced, menacing knives
and bullets, draping your living room
(that is, the room where you are supposed
to live) with sappy horrors dripping
merchandise and blood. A wall-to-wall
tease machine, to take the place of life.
Have you color in your scream?

BUTTERFLY

SOOT is New York's butterfly,
black, luminescent wings
gyrating in sunshine,
caught in a light shaft
between buildings.
More vital than the living,
its dazzle credible
for a moment. The monarch
flash of charred dead paper
that slowly flys to rest,
dissolving on our dirty
window panes.

DEATH OF A PRIZE POET

HE was the biggest con man I ever knew,
and conned himself right into insanity.
He beat up his wife, and wrote ten
brilliant pages about it, with several
endings, all of them published by the
quarrelling magazines; what a
slippery rationality was his.

But one trait was consistent;
he was mean, mean, mean—
and everyone could count on his
lack of humanity, which put him
right into the front lines of
the literary columns. People liked
his nasty candid view.

In floods of mixed-up paragraphs,
just crazy enough to possibly sound true,

he could talk you out of your mind, and
into his. The quality was genius,
with famous quotations peppering like footprints,
annotating the places he walked and
always ahead. It was, no doubt, too much
adrenalin, his ability to mow you down.
He sold himself, like soap, on exaggeration.

He fit into our civilization,
with drugs and drink and compulsion.
The next step, of course, was to die alone,
insane. This he did very well, providing
our shock and pain. For myself, personally,
enough to last a lifetime. My regret, though,
he wasn't here to read the Times obituary
    column.
Let not this final point seem cynicism.
I think he would have gleaned the social
    implication.
The facts are sad. It would have made a poem.

FOR THE WELL-DRESSED WOMEN
THROWING THEIR DIRTY PAPER TOWELS
ON THE REST ROOM FLOOR
AT THE METROPOLITAN MUSEUM

You are urbane, of no purpose or enchantment;
   willing to distribute waste like
the screwball catalysts (did they, against
   themselves, do it?) people dishonoring
their own gifts, the advantages, energy, time,
   and leaving idle dirt for others to clean.
Lautrec assembled that which you would have
   smeared,
      you provide the scrofula he made into art.

NEW COUPLES

WHAT can you do with coincidence?
sky with robin red meadows;
the outspread of green lawn shadows
approximating some thrush in elf dark.
I hear the hollow strokes of hermit love
lowering in the valley. Birds are like trees,
and a footstep cries to hillside; the musical
coherence that's on a flood dissolving. Grasses
are faint and silent, with unspoken magnification.
New couples are about, Vermeer girls with
    men Haitian-
black. I see them stroll beneath the lanterned
    night.

THERE IS NOW

THE closer to the bone, melancholy comes;
the price of seeing the shift,
ourselves a spangled drift,
witch grass hollows
each a deeper rose;
disaster's equipoise.
This contracts the mind
to sorrow's quiet blend,
toned melodies,
downed crickets in the wood.

The nearer to the cold,
this husk's deflowered gold
forges such organic threads of mourning,
there should be a song
to celebrate like spring.

There is now.
The high geese in the rain
igniting clouds
with raucous, happy
honks.

ON THE MEANING OF
LITERARY INFLUENCE

THERE are winners of prizes
who get most of their ideas
from half-known writers; it is
something like collectors
who dig in a back dusty store
and discover young Homer living
in rank, wilted pages nobody would
read, but the one who knows both
how to package and appreciate
good writing. Into his sagging
verse, he injects the scampered
music, and just unpretentious enough
to make the rhythm seem uneven,
and to strike the quartered measure.

Let us praise the famous writer
who unearths the faery gold.
As for the other crazy maker
with his rejects all unsold,
that's his function, to be a loser.
What he wins cannot be told.

CRITIC'S CHOICE

CRITICAL opinion is like mysticism,
comforting, sure-footed, adrift
in oblivion, but knowing the answers,
that is, telling; giving point
to whole worlds of stuff and fluff.
Plato on a cloud, sunsets maneuvering
up; I read the name-type of authors
and what a critic thinks of them,
and experience sweet certainty
in block print and phrases. Crinkling
open the Book Pages, I settle to
escape the cruel waves of fortune;
or better, watch from land
a sinking ship.

SKETCH BY STEPHEN CRANE

In our great current bovine, or simian,
world of excluding others for not
being ourselves, Crane won't give us
the swag excuse in any direction.
As in "An Eloquence in Grief"
the stereotype official (he perceives)
will always play it smart, and always
have in hand, behind his hand, the hidden
superior smile, and laughing
at fools who are drunk and forlorn.
And Stephen Crane shows us how our
    amusement
is a fatuous bone we've dug up, when starved
ourselves for shreds of humble grief.
Foul appetites he saw in men in 1899.
How will it be in 1981? Stupidity,
lusts, snide joys, go unforgiven!

IDENTITY CRISIS

ROBIN, do you know your name,
walking on the lawn? Sparrow
with your song intact, so inexact
as not to recite your species?
Garnet-headed woodpecker, quick
as flame, nailing your hard-billed
heart at sweet dry wood, why are you
not more smart, in blue morning
spring? And crows that bark,
and gold-blood finch aloft,
on Chinese paper wings tiny
as your music, why can't you
tell what half-struck bell
allows you to sing? To people,
you are dumb; your discourse
makes no claim, and trills pre-
cise far octaves, unexplained.

I WOULD RATHER

I WOULD rather you saved
the stones of Venice
than rocks from the moon.
"But what," you will say,
"does it mean? Saved,
destroyed?" And it will
take you a hundred years
to decide.

ALL evaporated, nobody real.
Yesterday was not so much better.
Then, I didn't try or exert.
When the good-looking couple
made nasty fun of cripples,
I thought, "oh well, the sins
of the world." I was an easy-going
snob. And the couple seemed to me
no more capable than worms.
I know now, they rule the ramparts
of the sky.

To evaporate is to die.
The standards are collapsed.
Jiggling puppets of wickedness
flay their victims, victims
flay their gods.

We are dawdling and obscene,
slaves to catastrophism.
(Nothing was intrinsic but desire.)
What is the difference to me?
My muscles ache like foam
bristling on the waters. Disillusion,
emptiness conjoin.

But I feel a raging impulse:
"Listen to me, world. *Now* you
must change."

DEDICATION IS AN EMBARRASSMENT
ONLY YOUR DREAMS CAN ADMIT

THE waves are blue and green,
and humanity is made of genes;
and people swing from wrong to wrong,
to right. The good ones aren't
the only smart intriguers; also evil
pulls on caste. But love is beyond,
and works for the impartial fates.

It is not that the last shall be first;
that's a pre-medicated concept. It is
that people of a fast conjunction,
and leaping against slow monsters,
will endeavor to exist and sometimes
with credible sport and gait; it is not
that a dictum dictates one against
the other. How befuddling is bad music,
imitating love and death, while the act
remains inimical, or cuts like jags in art
gouged out porches of place where life
slow travels. And it is not that the first,
or yet the last, will assemble in botched dia-
lectics. But that people do infer what yet
they have not seen; where yet they have not
been. The cold plunge into truth. The cure
that first was dreamed is true; but changed.

AGAINST POETRY AS ADVERTISING

You are right.
Poetry is advertising.
Except, the ingredients are different;
where subtleties are held, unencumbered,
and intelligence is not dismembered;
and what to buy is dismissed
for strange avail.

But, you are right.
Poetry is advertising.
And Valéry abdicated
when he took up mathematics;
though, not defecting to the infinite zeroes;
and he abolished all numbering credos.
Each essence, he proposed, like love
was incalculable.

But now, you say, that's archaic.
And in times of revolution
poetry must be advertising,
crunching up the process
with the goal.
And no place for the sensitive action,
or even Valéry's crazy tolerant fractions.
Albeit, true insurgence
was never a slogan;
but, viable.

TRACING BACK

My mother took care of my father's shirts;
he did not take care of her cotton dresses.
I think he would have been ashamed,
not of the labor, but of a peculiar
sense of squalor, a man wasting his time,
winding his arms around the soiled garments,
the daily plethora, and humble sheddings.
What grim, unpresiding angel, drooped and dull?
Both of them, a part of the aboriginal pool.

PRE-CONDITIONS

THE naked will is too covered.
Which means the opposite to what it means;
and standing up to be counted was the bottom
of pretend, like children seeing first by what's
imagined. But you didn't have to fake it,
the contrapuntal mulch, strawy to the touch
and light and warm. Spirit! you never could
have existed without the private person.
So, the big muscle warp was never true,
the ideal roaring gang that wanted a fight.
What you live for and declare, and now you
    know it,
is something that felt delicious, and happened in
    quiet.

THE SUBWAY CHURCH

THE subway is the church
where all our eyes ride level
comprehending good and evil;
blood squeezed to its extreme.
No false rhetoric, to lead.
But foot-jawed out of hell,
and sharp angels of control
holding back some final
human horror. Each measured
on his own, and the scream
of the tracks is a sermon.
Ancient, flea-bag shy ones
wait their turn; or a criminal
takes command. And heroes must
adroitly turn to secretly be kind.

The soul is stretched beyond
to what suffering cannot mend.
In all eyes we see the truth,
and hold the truth in hand.
Underneath this hard damned earth,
the subway is the church.

PLUMS AND PEARS

In their dreams they do things
that others do really—
in their dreams it is real.

And those who do it really
feel as if they have been
living in dreams.

SIGRID, KEEPER OF THE *JOTUNHEIM INN*

You lived like your sea captain husband
riding the cold swindle of the reassuring waves,
the Norwegian preachers in the storm clouds
you expedited with good health;
you lived in your topmast castle,
and the loneliness of introverted smashings,
so when he came back and retired,
and strode the vast lawn screaming for Bjornson
poet of childhood, and God's injustice
    remembered,
you brought little decks of calm to assuage.
But he died. And, so now have you.
Widow of the Jotunheim mountains,
crests of Ibsen burning within you,
and like St. Olaf's pilgrims.

When I was twenty-one, Mr. John Esthetique
   Upsom
turned down my poems, he said, because
they were too hung up on social revolution.
When I was thirty-two, the Mountain College
   Review
turned down my poems, they said, because
they were too much a part of some literary
   milieu.
When I was forty, the Barricades Quarterly
turned down my poems, they said,
because I was forty.

ON STIMULATION, BY DEGRADATION

(After seeing swingy travel article,
"Hire a Girl for the Night.")

THEY feed us like a shoe in the mouth,
a kick in the jaw. It appeals,
it conceals, it holds back tomorrow.
Hiring a woman to be a lackey,
(crushing slaves into a matrix
of blackie) it rhymes in the mind
of no mind. Yet, the sorrowing patience
of those who will not menace, or enjoy
the comedy of constitutional injustice—
they file past us, with no backward smiles.

So you think you are moving
on silky carpets of metaphysics;
but there are many more conglomerate
forces moving, and the wide streets
impel single people to act outside
caste system feeling; and no definition
can hold them into what you dream
is the planned skull bone of a god.
And the filmy waitress women are not dis-
charging like common numbers; they rise
and sway and punch factories in the jaw,
and tell injustice to cease; and the stocky,
unhappy people you think are but folding
   elbows,
conjoining against the beauty you admire, I say
to you, they are made of it. You see too much
on the surface, the dark night waits beyond;

and you, who love the future, just admit
the gold drop on each tongue. You have said
that truth is never plain, and meanwhile
you shrivel it down; forgetting the myriad
factors, and in the shape of the toiling crowd,
yourself walking among.

PEDRO AT BASEBALL

PLAYING the field, glinting black eyes
under a cap so sharp, it is like your
sharp feelings, an arrow from Puerto Rico
delivered across the skies. I think of
your glinting eyes, and the honey-sweet
mango boughs; two children and a wife, they
are tropical Catholics. And their lives
like glinted leaves, with the bright sun
pouring on; but they live in dirty Brooklyn
in the slums. In the day you bring the
laundry, at night you play your baseball.
The klieg lights baking southern in the
mud. "I'm never tired," you say. "I am
happy with my family." You trudge the
lousy street, hoisting the heavy packages.
"I like it," you say. "Good exercise."

THE FULCRUM

Vɪᴇᴛɴᴀᴍ is the fulcrum,
   the support of resistant branches;
and in our strong sixth sense we detect,
   without pathos, the balance has come
upon us to say *enough*. Disasters, sadism,
   who can prescribe from deep poisons?
But so famous are the crass irrationals
   and history imbibing horror, and war
the profitable error, inertia locked in chaos
   bullies us down. In our strong sixth
sense, we perceive it. Nations riding up
   to the round, no greedy great can match
the power of victims. Vietnam is the fulcrum,
   the fixed point, divisible. Old fist
of the mind, give in, dissolve, compound......

FOR THE GIFTED

So well anointed with cleverness and
   contempt,
I think you can afford to hate what you do,
reject what you love, erase what was splendor,
slash the picture you worked at so long.
You are rich and emboldened by what the world
   gives,
demanding the high moment on which you can
   spit.
There is something glorious, I know, almost
   volcanic
about the churn, and broken chains; elements of
   reversal.
You can afford it. As for me, I walk a poor road
picking up pebbles for the brains in my head.

One, two, three, I am polishing and holding.
Such ideas, perhaps, I prize because nobody else
   wants them.
From auras that you squander, I catch some little
   bit.
My work seems very hard, valuable. I can't
   help it.

MILLENNIUM

W<small>HEN</small> courtesy will be the new energy,
fronded and spangled, limpid and free,
bursting like mirrors catching reflections,
truthful to love, that brisk discipline,
truthful to death, that unwavering hurt,
truthful to life, expanding like thought,
when courtesy's the bomb, more brilliant than
    fire,
the talented listener, the retroactive conductor,
no pipe lines to rage, but rippling flowers
in waves of comprehension, when courtesy splits
    open
our dung heaps of hate, and like pollens
    updrifted,
and willows in light, we become drunken,
    ecstatic—
and all will be changed, multivascular, forgiving,

in new ring stratas of living, whorls within
    whorls
and air for high breathing; the conscience, the
    care,
consolidating like engines, like angels, and
    melting
the mean cause and fear. When courtesy will be
the new energy, and the curtain goes up on
    power
opt from pleasure; and each hovering soul
    knowing,
to save and protect the root dark of living,
before existence is stomped out . . . .

TALENT

HAVING no talent is the new talent.
Keeping your brains under a pat of dust,
sighting islands in glazed eyeballs,
and roaring down the street, dead stupid.
The new elite is in holding back on ideas,
tying them up like unhappy dogs,
until they grow timid, or crazy.
Leave out feeling, love and surprise,
and keep it blunt and devoid of purpose
but join, join and join in with the new
gray couriers of no music, all together now,
oh, monolith monotone . . . .

WISDOM AND WORK,
AS YET UNHEARD MUSIC

THE melding, out of social abysses,
    the welding of broken spaces,
and the crew permanence of people
    who work, these are not
playing to the enervations
    of crossed purposes.
The rose mirage of late colors
    is being told, and of wisdom
in despair. And those who sigh
    too loud, and praise, are still
yet but echoes, and memories of the lost
    air ventricles. Even the old
are the blessing of youth; and even
    the false murmurers will yet
adhere to truth. Let wisdom be silent;
    and music, extant, follow after.

THE HUMAN ANIMAL

To make me do the thing I will, I won't.
Facing front, it's back I turn
to scorn the right intent.
The worse I am, the better do. Against
my own impulse I plot; and overthrown
rise up to govern all I have undone.

To live my life, I've lost it. Or reversed,
the greatest loss was living most;
the best I did was least.
By counter causes, grown then capable,
I've come to some short pass. And passing still,
go on to learn what's gone; and what I will.

PRINTED AT

THE STINEHOUR PRESS